Enjoy the picture of the
Gatineau ~CROSS~
never old CROSS
love
Maurie Dawn.
Thanks to
S0-AAB-205

OUT OUR BACK DOOR

Revealing Photographs and Inspirational
Thoughts That Nourish the Soul

Ed Soup

Introduction

Nature, when you really take the time to look and listen, provides powerful messages for us to ponder. We have lived in Wakefield since 1985 and hardly a day goes by when we are not moved by the beauty it has to offer.

We regularly witness, out the back door of our house, intervals of time when we are left in awe of nature's artistry and many years ago we began to capture these special occurrences on film. We soon realized it would be a great gift to share with others if we put this collection of photos together in book form and accompanied each inspiring moment with the messages we felt they were conveying to us.

We literally discovered acres of diamonds in our back yard. Even though the book is only a small sample of the many photographs which capture the natural beauty of Wakefield, we sincerely hope you will enjoy them as much as we do.

We are grateful to you for purchasing this book and helping us plant seeds, so to speak, throughout the world. We hope that these seeds will sprout and, eventually, produce blossoms of great understanding, respect and love — for yourself, for others and for this wonderful planet that all of us call home.

Let us continue to work together to take better care of Mother Earth so that our children and theirs can enjoy it tomorrow as much as we do today.

We invite you to come visit our scenic village if you have not already done so, and to visit it again if you have been here before. Wakefield is nestled on the banks of the Gatineau River in the Gatineau Hills just a half hour from Ottawa, our Nation's Capital. Come and see for yourself the beauty and tranquillity that our village has to offer. Our back door awaits you.

Enjoy!!
Ed and Gaye Chicoine

Gaye Chicoine is a photographer by profession, but a home-schooling mother by reality. She captured these special moments at all times of the day and in all seasons — sometimes at 5 A.M., sometimes at 20 degrees below zero, and sometimes during a mid-summer morning sunrise.

Ed Chicoine is a chiropractor. His contribution is the insights that accompany these photographs.

P.S. As previously stated and as incredible as it may seem, all the photographs in this book were taken "out the back door" of our home.

This special and beautiful moment in nature existed for only a few seconds when captured by camera.

Hunches, feelings, inspirations and revelations all occur in a flash. When we capture them, our lives can be changed forever.

There is a new world waiting outside of our present self. We need only to move forward.

Stand out among the crowd

Be a leader

No statues were ever erected for someone
who simply followed the crowd

Never compare yourself or compete with others
for there will always be some who are greater or
lesser than you

Greet each morning with gratitude
for the gift of another day

Count your blessings,
don't add up your troubles
and don't take life too seriously.
Nobody comes out of it alive

The earth shine illuminates
the dark side of the moon

We should reflect our love, happiness
and positive feelings
to illuminate the hearts of others

Forgiveness cures more hearts than surgery

The greatest force in the universe
is unconditional love

We need to put up bridges, not walls to help foster positive relationships with our neighbors

When we do our best to help others in our community, it has an impact on the rest of the world

Communities are parts of towns and cities, which in turn are parts of the provinces and states that make up countries, continents, and ultimately our planet

Think globally, act locally

The sun still shines even behind cloud cover

There is always something positive
behind troubled times

Hardships are like weights:
They strengthen our bodies and our spirits

The person that never makes a mistake
never makes a discovery

Circumstances
don't make a person,
they reveal them

Success
is something that you attract
by who you are

Your true self
is like a source of light
and it wants you to shine
so you can find
your true identity

Nature never works hard,
worries or tries:
It simply is and abundance comes

First you have to be,
before you do,
before you have

Be that special someone
who advances confidently
in the direction of your dreams.
Do what you truly love to do.
Have lasting inner peace

We are part of the perfection of nature

Following nature's laws allows us to live
the higher life

Natural laws cannot be broken.
We only break ourselves
if we do not follow them

The morning dew silently presents itself.
Its moisture is capable of sustaining life

We should strive
to have a quiet mind

Don't seek happiness — Create it

It is said that a butterfly
flapping its wings in one continent
can effect the wind currents in another

Everything you say or do makes a difference

Attitudes are contagious.
Is yours worth catching?

Nature vibrates with energy to produce endless beauty

Likewise, your positive thoughts vibrate with energy
to produce your heart's desire

To truly appreciate the rainbow
you must be willing to stand in the rain

If you plant enough flowers,
the weeds won't grow

No matter what happens in life,
being anything other than cheerful
will not make it better

Personal growth
is just as natural for human beings
as it is for flowers
to turn their faces to the sun

When you are inspired by a life mission,
special forces will come to your aid

You will discover talents you thought you never had
and your mind will transcend all limitations

You will create your destiny

We are all equally part of the universe:
One verse, one song

The sun rises and sets for every human being
regardless of skin color, religion,
nationality or language

We are all equal and interconnected
in the eyes of God

What comes from the sun are rays of light
because that is what it is made of

If negativity, deceitfulness, anger,
fear and resentment come out of you,
then obviously they are inside, part of you

The only way that negative thoughts
can have any power over you is if you listen to them

Stop the self-sabotage

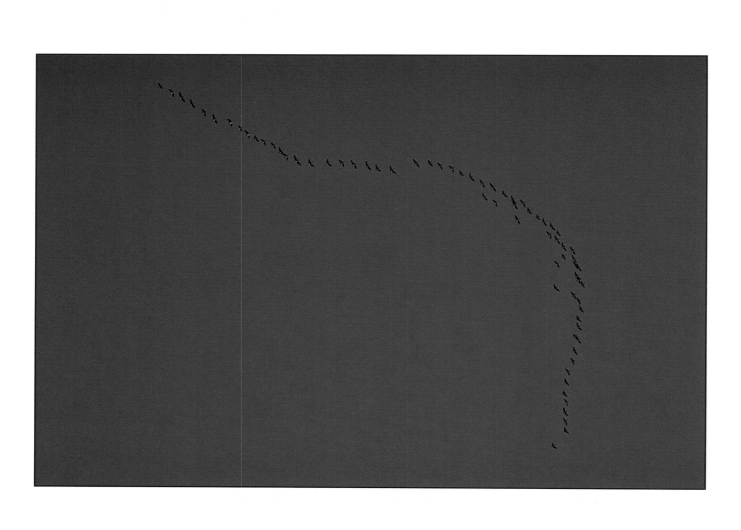

As each goose flaps its wings, it creates an uplift for the bird immediately following. By flying in V formation, the flock has 71 percent greater flying range than if each bird flew on its own.

When the head goose gets tired it rotates back in the wing and another goose flies point. Geese honk from behind to encourage those up front.

When a goose falls out of formation due to sickness or an injury, two other geese fall out with the wounded bird to help and protect it. They stay with the fallen goose until it is able to fly…or it dies.

If we had the sense of a goose, we would stand by each other in good times and bad, share a common direction and sense of community, take turns doing demanding jobs, and cheer each other on when the going gets tough.

Taking the path of least resistance
is what makes rivers crooked

Having a clear, precise goal
is like eliminating
the curves and banks in the river

Stand for something
or you'll fall for anything

The Earth is dynamic

Because of its movement we experience beauty:
In the sunrises, sunsets, and seasons

Dynamic people
experience dynamic lives

You can never step into the same river twice

The past is gone and the future is promised to no one

All you have is now

How good are you at living in the present moment?

It is the key to manifesting miracles in your life

We get a much better perspective on life when we widen our vision

Wondrous things can be seen when we truly take the time to observe and look at the whole picture, instead of seeing things through the filter of our own perceptions and judgements

When we lose negative emotions, opinions and judgements, our minds expand

The sun provides selfless service to humankind

It provides light, heat, life energy
and never asks anything in return

You cannot hold a torch
to light another's path
without brightening your own

I would rather put my faith and trust in the force
that is capable of creating such beauty and abundance

When it comes to my life, health, and happiness,
I would rather follow nature's laws

Even the educated mind cannot surpass
our innate natural wisdom

*Nature exists harmoniously and in balance
within the duality of life*

North — South / East — West / Night — Day

*When the spiritual and physical become one,
life is limitless*

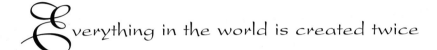Everything in the world is created twice

First in the imagination or dreams,
and then in reality

Never underestimate
the power of the mind

Albert Einstein said,
"Dreams are more powerful than knowledge"

There is order in the universe

Winter always follows autumn and so on

Self-renewal and self-transformation are indeed
possible. The proof is given everyday in nature

Allow real life to come in and move you up
and away from your old nature

If we want to enjoy the beauty and glory of the sunrise, we must go through the night

Peace of mind does not come from the absence of conflict, but from our ability to cope with it

Each one of us has four dimensions:
Spiritual, Mental, Emotional, and Physical

Their interconnectedness is what makes us whole,
which is another word for health

To be truly whole we must connect
to all four dimensions

The dawn of a new day
brings with it limitless possibilities

You may not be able
to change your destination overnight
but you can change your direction

No matter how dark the situation may be,
raise your sights and see the possibilities

Only light can drive out darkness.
Only right action on your part
can drive out the wrongness in your life

The same forces that created this beautiful forest from tiny seeds flow through you as well

If you carefully examine those seeds, even under a powerful microscope, it is impossible to detect the life force they hold: The power to create mighty trees

There is something that is very much a part of you that is invisible: Your soul and spirit

How connected are you to your internal spiritual forces?

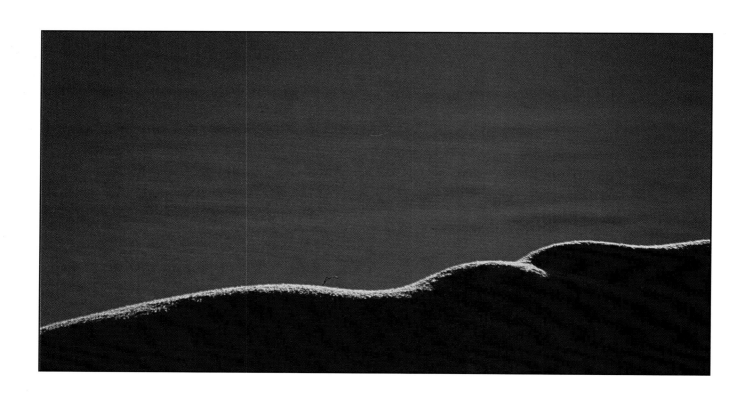

Like the snow which gets molded and shaped
according to the external forces imposed upon it,
we must humble ourselves to the power
of the universe, nature or God

We are here to serve and love others
for the benefit of humankind

Do this and everything else falls into place

If the universe has given you a dream
or a strong desire to achieve a worthy goal,
it is because you already possess
the innate ability to achieve it

All knowledge is always known and ever present

It is simply a matter of tuning into it

Nature works in cycles

There is a time of great production
and a time of rest

The winter of life
is a time to go inside and reflect on oneself,
to improve inner awareness
and self-understanding

To be more effective and productive,
sculptors always take the time necessary
to sharpen their tools

There is no such thing as miracles in life,
only unknown natural forces

The more we advance in science and knowledge
the more we realize what we don't know

We cannot deny the existence of some things
just because they cannot be seen or measured

600 years ago people believed
that the earth was flat

We did not know cells existed
until the invention of the microscope

If we wait for science
to explain everything before we believe,
we will miss out on many of the existing possibilities

The power that rotates the earth, moves the seas,
gives life, and takes it away is everything

Connect to that power

About the Authors

Ed Chicoine was born in Haileybury, and Gaye Michlowski Chicoine was born in Sudbury, both in the province of Ontario. They went to the same high-school in the small town of Chelmsford.

After graduating from Fanshawe College of Photography in 1977, Gaye worked as a commercial photographer and part-time college teacher. Ed obtained a Bachelor of Physical and Health Education degree from the University of Toronto in 1979, and graduated from the Canadian Memorial Chiropractic College in 1983.

Ed and Gaye were married in 1983 and then spent their honeymoon travelling for six months across Japan, Hong Kong, Thailand, Nepal, Singapore, Australia, New Zealand and Fiji. Their first child was born in Ottawa in 1984. They moved to Wakefield, Québec in 1985, where their five other children were born at home. Ed continues to operate a chiropractic practice to serve the people of Wakefield and the surrounding area.

In January, 1997 they left on a family adventure with their six children driving from Canada to the bottom of South America and back. During their three-and-a-half-year odyssey, they crossed through 13 different countries. On their 11 month return trip from Chile to Canada they mostly camped, sleeping in tents, hammocks and on the ground. Observing and photographing a wide array of landscapes and sceneries sharpened their sense of awareness and made them feel more connected to the earth.

Upon their return to Wakefield, they had a new and different perspective. The nature that surrounded them seemed more vibrant and alive than ever. The result was the creation of this book.